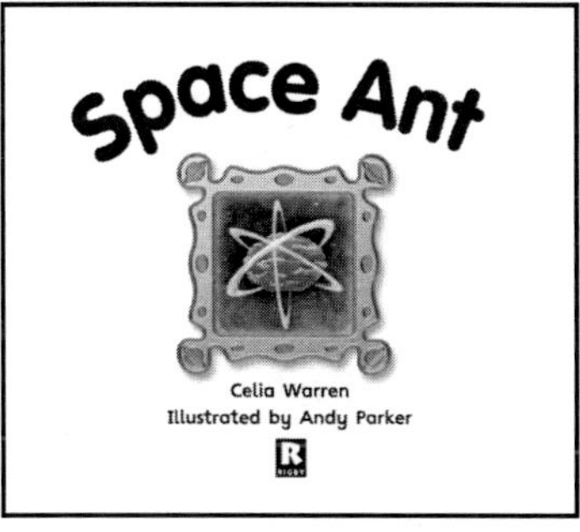

Walkthrough

Look at the picture on the cover.

Where do you think this story is set?

This is Space Ant, and she's lost.

Do you like Space Ant's spaceship?

In the story she goes to visit some planets and meets some creatures.

Walkthrough

Let's read the blurb together.

Who do you think she will meet?

Walkthrough

Let's read the title.

These are the author's and illustrator's names. This is the publisher's logo.

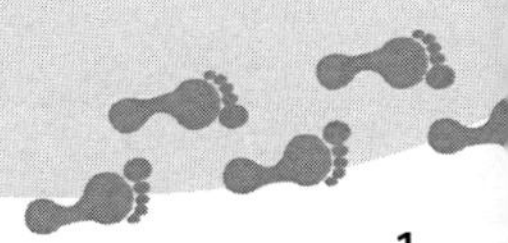

Walkthrough

Space Ant is lost.

She's looking at a map.

She wants to go home to her own planet.

She says, 'There's no place like home.' What do you think this means?

 **Observe and Prompt**

Word Recognition

- Check the children can read the words 'Space', 'place' and 'came' using their decoding skills. Help them with the vowel sounds (from 'a' and silent 'e') if they have difficulty. You might like to point out the silent 'e' in 'home' too.

- Help the children with the 'ue' sound in 'blue' if they struggle.

- Check the children can read the word 'planet' using their decoding skills. Can they read the adjacent consonants at the beginning of this word?

What colour is the planet Space Ant can see?

Do you think Space Ant will go and have a look
at the blue planet?

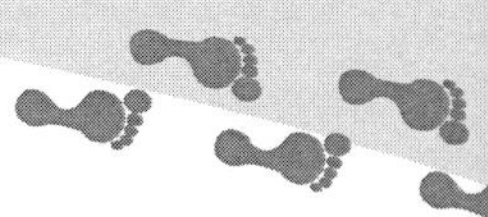

 **Observe and Prompt**

Language Comprehension

- Observe the children reading with expression, especially
  when reading speech.
- Check the children understand the expression 'There's no
  place like home'.
- Ask the children which planet Space Ant came to.
- What do the children think the blue planet will be like?

Walkthrough

How does Ant feel on the planet?

How can you tell she's cold?

What sound does she make? (*Brrrr*)

 Observe and Prompt

Word Recognition

- If the children have difficulty reading 'freezing', ask them if they recognise the adjacent consonants at the beginning of this word, then prompt for blending through the word.

- If the children have difficulty reading 'tigeroo', prompt them to break the word down into three syllables before blending the whole word together.

- If the children have difficulty reading 'Isn't', model the reading of this word for them.

Walkthrough

This is a tigeroo.

How does the tigeroo feel?

Does the tigeroo like it on the blue planet?

 ## Observe and Prompt

Language Comprehension

- Check the children are reading with expression, especially the words 'Brrr' and 'Yesss'.

- Ask the children which two animals they think the tigeroo is like.

- Do the children think the tigeroo likes the blue planet? Why not?

Walkthrough

What do you think Space Ant said to the tigeroo?

Do you think Space Ant likes the tigeroo?

 **Observe and Prompt**

Word Recognition

- If the children have difficulty reading 'another', prompt them to break the word down into three syllables, before blending the whole word together.

- Check the children can read 'went', 'Let's' and 'they' using their decoding skills.

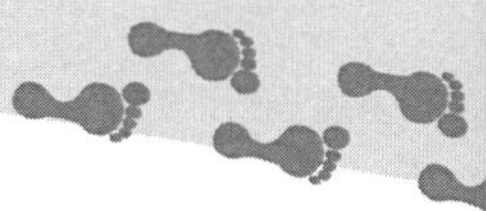

Off they went.
Next, they came to a red planet.
"Let's go and have a look," they said.

7

 **Observe and Prompt**

Language Comprehension

- Ask the children which planet Space Ant and tigeroo came
  to next.

- What do the children think this planet will be like?

- Do the children think they will like this planet?

 **Observe and Prompt**

Word Recognition

- If the children have difficulty reading 'Phew', ask them if they recognise the initial letters and sound 'Ph', then help them with the vowel sound – 'ew'.

- Model the blending of the word 'boiling' if the children struggle.

- If the children have difficulty reading 'Along', prompt them to split the word into two syllables, before blending the word together from left to right.

- Prompt the children to break the word 'elebird' down into three syllables, before blending the whole word together.

Walkthrough

This is an elebird.

How do you think the elebird is feeling?

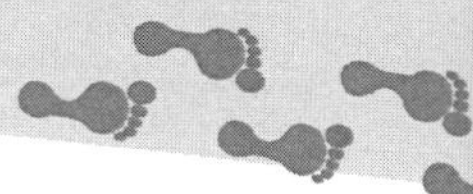

Along came an elebird.
"Hello," said the tigeroo. "Isn't it hot here?"
"It's **too** hot," said the elebird. "I don't like it here."

9

 **Observe and Prompt**

Language Comprehension

- Check the children are reading with appropriate expression.
- Ask the children which two animals the children think the elebird is a cross between.
- Ask the children if they think the creatures like the red planet.

Walkthrough

What do you think Space Ant is saying to
the elebird?

How do you think the tigeroo feels?

 ## Observe and Prompt

Word Recognition

- Check the children can read the word 'zoomed' using their
  decoding skills. If they have difficulty, help them with the
  'ed' suffix at the end of the word.

- Check the children can read the adjacent consonants in the
  words 'past' and 'stars'.

- You may need to help the children with the 'le' sound in
  'purple' if this has not yet been taught.

Walkthrough

They zoomed past lots of stars.

Then what did the tigeroo, the elebird and Space Ant
see from the spaceship?

What do you think they'll do?

What do you think this planet will be like?

 **Observe and Prompt**

Language Comprehension

- Ask the children which planet the friends are going to now.
- What do the children think the purple planet will be like?
- Do the children think they will like the purple planet?

Walkthrough

What is the purple planet like?

Is it too hot?

Is it too cold?

Do you think Space Ant and her friends
like it?

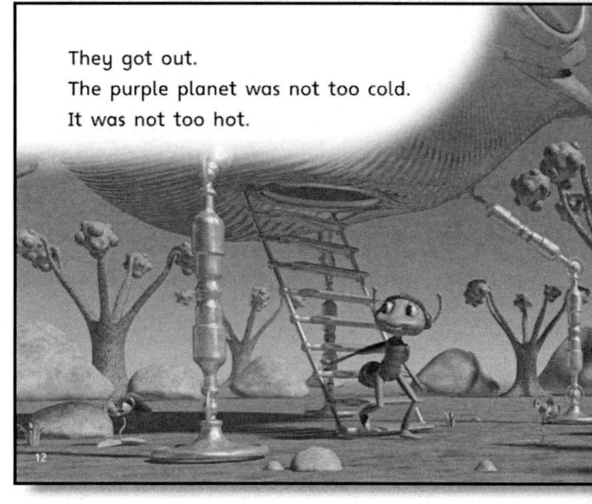

Observe and Prompt

Word Recognition

- Check the children can read the CVC words 'got', 'not' and 'hot' confidently.

- Check the children can read the sight words 'out', 'was' and 'too'.

- Check the children can read 'They', 'planet' and 'cold' more confidently using their decoding skills.

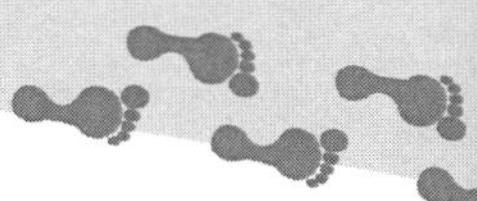

 **Observe and Prompt**

Walkthrough

Do you think the tigeroo and elebird like the
purple planet?

How can you tell?

 **Observe and Prompt**

Word Recognition

- Check the children can read 'just' using their decoding skills.

- If the children have difficulty reading 'right', model the blending of this word for them.

- Check the children can read the word 'love' using their decoding skills. If they have difficulty, help them with the vowel' sound (from 'o' and silent 'e').

- Model the reading of 'because' if the children have difficulty with this word.

 **Observe and Prompt**

Language Comprehension

- Check for expressive reading appropriate to the punctuation and emboldened text.
- Ask the children what the tigeroo and elebird think of the purple planet.
- Ask the children why the Space Ant loves the purple planet.
- Do the children think they would like to visit the purple planet?

Walkthrough

Who are all these creatures?

Are they pleased to see Space Ant, the elebird and the tigeroo?

What does Space Ant say?

"There's no place like home!"

 **Observe and Prompt**

Language Comprehension

- Observe fluent, expressive reading.
- Ask the children what Space Ant says in the end.
- How do the children think Space Ant feels?

16